Meringue
Girls*

Published by Square Peg 2013

2 4 6 8 10 9 7 5 3 1

First published in Great Britain in 2013 by
Square Peg
Random House, 20 Vauxhall Bridge Road,
London SW1V 2SA

www.randomhouse.co.uk

Addresses for companies within The Random House Group Limited can be found at:
www.randomhouse.co.uk/offices.htm

The Random House Group Limited Reg. No. 954009

A CIP catalogue record for this book
is available from the British Library

ISBN 9780224096003

Photography: David Loftus
Design: Well Made Studio
Food styling: Alex Hoffler and Stacey O'Gorman
Prop styling: Jo Harris
Illustrated titles and paint washes: Kenn Goodall

Printed and bound in China by C&C Offset Printing Co.,Ltd.

Meringue
Girls x

SQUARE PEG

**This book has
interactive content**

Download the free
Layar App

Find and scan pages
with the Layar logo

Discover
video content

THIS BOOK IS DEDICATED TO
EVERYONE WHO DREAMS
OF LEAVING THEIR 9 TO 5.

introduction

Introduction

Cupcakes, cake pops
and macarons have had
their day. Now is the age
of the meringue.

Meringue Girls are making meringues cool again! We handcraft the best meringues you have ever tasted: mallowy in the middle, with a melt-in-the-mouth texture.

In this book we aim to demystify meringues, which are notoriously hard to make. We will show you the easy way to ensure fail-proof meringues every time.

We'll share our fresh, modern and colourful take on classic meringue recipes, giving them a Meringue Girls twist with exciting flavour combinations.

Our book includes heaps of gift ideas, fun ways to get the kids involved, easy and impressive summer dessert ideas and indulgent winter dinner party puddings.

OUR MERINGUES
ARE NATURALLY
GLUTEN FREE.

WE ARE BIG ON FLAVOUR.
THE POSSIBILITIES ARE ENDLESS
- JUST USE YOUR 'WILLY
WONKA' CREATIVE FLAIR.

pistachio

raspberry

chocolate

70% chocolate...

vanilla

WE RECOMMEND USING THE BEST-QUALITY NATURAL INGREDIENTS,

SUCH AS FREE-RANGE EGG WHITES, BRITISH-GROWN SUGAR AND 70% DARK CHOCOLATE AND COCOA.

ABOUT THE MERINGUE GIRLS

Alex Hoffler

Alex is London born and bred. Following university and two years working at a major London marketing agency, she travelled for a year, taking cookery courses in India, Thailand, Cambodia and Vietnam.

She then completed a year's course at Leiths School of Food and Wine, where she received a first class diploma. She currently does food styling for various publications.

Stacey O'Gorman

Growing up in Auckland, New Zealand, from a young age Stacey had a passion for food. She trained at Auckland University of Technology achieving a Diploma in Culinary Arts.

To widen her experience, Stacey took a year out to explore the culinary world, honing her skills in kitchens along the way. In one such kitchen she met Alex, with whom she shared an epicurean passion, and a partnership was born.

The Girls

Trained chefs Alex and Stacey formed the Meringue Girls after working together in a restaurant in Hackney. They bonded over a love of sweet things, especially meringues. From big launches and pop-ups to weddings and gift boxes, they have worked with amazing clients including **Vogue Night Out**, **Whistles**, **Jimmy Choo**, **L'Oreal**, **H&M**, **Elle** and **Marie Claire**.

But they keep their feet firmly on the ground and love to show up at street food events including **FEAST**, **KERB**, **Street Feast**, Jamie Oliver's **Fifteen Market**, Gizzi Erskine's **K-Town** and **Chilli Stand Off**. They also supply **Selfridges** and **Harvey Nichols** in London.

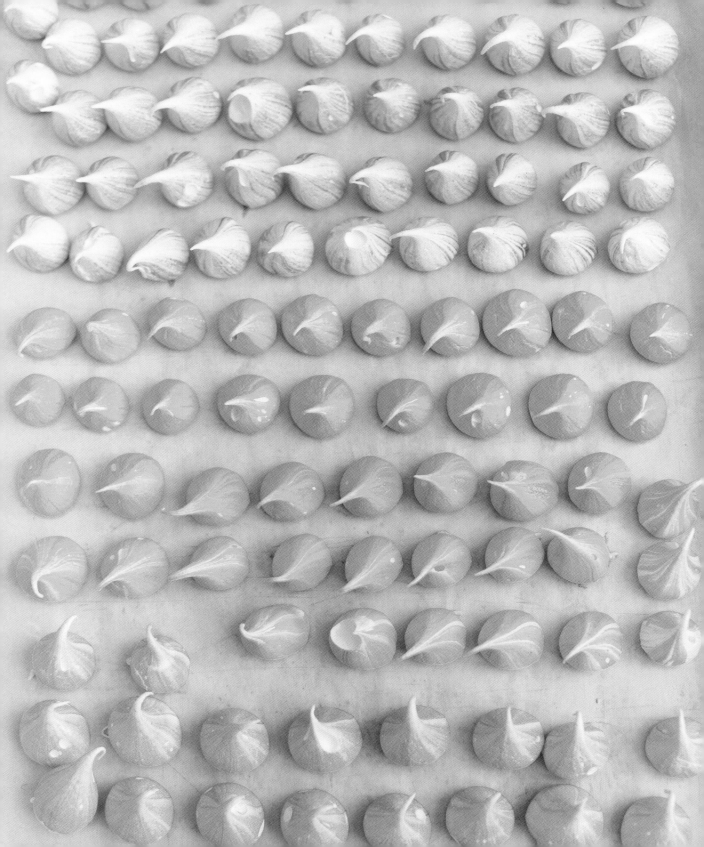

TIPS AND TECHNIQUES

Meringues are all about volume!

Here are some points to remember to ensure maximum voluminosity.

A free-standing mixer is your best friend (we use a Kitchen Aid mixer), but it is also possible to make meringues with a handheld electric whisk. Hand whisking is fine for making small batches (3 egg whites max. for us), but for larger amounts you'll need big biceps and a lot of willpower.

Use clean equipment. Greasy bowls and utensils will deflate the lovely volume you have created. We often wipe out our mixing bowl with lemon juice to make double sure it's spotless. Grease tends to cling to plastic bowls and spatulas, so stick to metal or glass ones.

Make sure whites are free from yolk and shell – crack them carefully and check the whites before you start to whisk. The best way to get rid of a split yolk is to use a bit of shell to fish it out.

The biggest pitfall with meringue making is adding the sugar before the whites are totally stiff. If you add sugar too early, your meringues will never acquire the stiff consistency you want.

Volume is made by stretching the elasticity of the egg whites to their full capacity. The whites are stiff enough when you can hold the bowl upside down without them dropping out.

We use caster sugar for most meringue methods as the fine grain dissolves in the mixture very quickly. We heat our sugar so that it dissolves even quicker, giving a smooth and glossy mixture. If the sugar hasn't been allowed to dissolve and the mixture is grainy when it goes into the oven, the meringues will often leak a sugar syrup during baking.

Meringues can be covered in cling film or placed in an airtight container and stored in a cool, dry place for up to 2 weeks. Do not refrigerate.

We use free-range liquid egg whites, which work really well – and we don't have 500 yolks swimming in our fridge the way we used to. Two Chicks free-range egg whites is a great brand to try.

Golden caster sugar gives a lovely caramel taste and appearance to meringues. Substitute in any recipe.

Vinegar lends a chewiness to meringues. Add ½ a tsp to your stiff whites for a really mallowy middle

Cream of tartar stabilises your whites and makes a stiffer but less glossy mixture. Use when your egg whites are getting old.

MERINGUE GIRLS MIXTURE

Our meringue to sugar ratio is very easy to remember – it is double the amount of sugar to egg whites. A medium egg white weighs 30g – so use 60g of caster sugar per egg. *Always weigh your whites as eggs vary in size.*

MAKES ABOUT 35 KISSES

150g free-range
 egg whites
 (5 medium eggs)
300g caster sugar

Start by lining a large baking sheet with baking paper.

Preheat the oven to 200°C/gas 6. Line a roasting tray with baking paper, pour in the caster sugar and put in the oven for about 5 minutes until the edges are just beginning to melt. Heating the sugar will help it dissolve in the egg whites more quickly to create a glossy, stable mixture.

Meanwhile, weigh your egg whites in your free-standing mixer bowl, or a non-plastic bowl. Make sure your bowl and whisk are free from grease. Whisk slowly at first, allowing small stabilising bubbles to form, then increase the speed until the egg whites form stiff peaks, and the bowl can be tipped upside down without the egg falling out.

Keep an eye on the mixture and stop whisking just before it turns into a cotton woolly appearance, at which point the mixture will be over-whisked and will have lost some of its elasticity in the egg white protein.

At this point, the sugar should be ready to take out of the oven. Turn your oven down to 100°C/gas ¼. Leave the door ajar to speed up the cooling.

With the whites stiff and while whisking again at full speed, add one big tablespoon of the hot sugar after another to the meringue mixture, ensuring that it comes back up to stiff peaks after each spoonful of sugar. Don't worry about any small clumps of sugar, but avoid any larger chunks of caremelized sugar from the edges of the roasting tray.

Once you have added all of the sugar, continue to whisk on full speed for about 5-7 minutes. Feel a bit of the mixture between your fingers, and if you can still feel the gritty sugar, keep whisking at full speed until the sugar has dissolved and the mixture is smooth, and the bowl is a little cooler to the touch. The mixture will continue to thicken up during this stage. You know when it is ready to use when it forms a nice smooth, shiny peak on the tip of your upturned finger.

To find out how to colour, flavour and pipe your meringues, flick over to page 30.

Once you have assembled your meringues in your desired shapes and sizes on a baking tray lined with baking paper (leaving a couple of centimetres between each shape), they will bake in an oven set to 100°C/gas ¼.

Bite-sized kisses (see next page) should be baked for approximately 30-40 minutes. Take them out of the oven as soon as they easily lift off the baking paper with their bases intact.

For larger meringues (like nests), bake for 2 hours, or if you are doing even larger pavlovas, bake for 3 hours. (You can turn the oven off and leave for a few more hours or overnight if you want them to dry out further.)

When the meringues are cooked, leave them to cool on the baking sheet.

These will keep well for 2 weeks, covered with cling film or placed in an airtight container and stored in a cool, dry place.

COLOURING, PIPING AND FLAVOURING KISSES

Colouring

Meringue kisses are a fun way to shape and colour meringues. You can use them in a variety of different desserts, cake tiers and petits fours. All our meringue kisses are hand piped, bite-sized, and each has its own unique organic shape and colour.

To colour the kisses, make a batch of uncooked Meringue Girls Mixture *(see p.26)*, and turn a piping bag inside out. Place the bag over a jug or bottle so that it holds itself up. Using natural food colouring and a clean paintbrush, paint thick stripes from the tip of your piping bag to halfway down the bag (about 5 stripes).

Then carefully spoon your stiff meringue mixture into the piping bag and turn it the right side out.

You need to pack the meringue mixture in tightly, ensuring there are no air bubbles.

With sharp scissors, cut the tip of the piping bag to the size of a 20p coin.

To get the piping bag flowing, use some of the mixture to pipe small dollops onto the 4 corners of your baking sheets (if you are doing a full batch of 35 kisses you will need a couple of baking sheets), and use like glue to stick your baking paper to the sheet.

You are ready to start piping!

Piping

Hold the piping bag with both hands, placing your dominant hand at the top of the piping bag and your other hand halfway down the bag. Use the top hand to apply pressure and the lower hand to control the flow of the kisses. Squeeze the bag (like an udder!) to form the kisses. They should have a 5cm diameter and a big peak at the top. This takes practice, so don't worry if you don't get it right the first time.

You can use different nozzles for different effects. For example, a star nozzle will give you beautiful little star-like kisses.

Flavouring

Traditionally, meringues have simply been flavoured with chocolate, vanilla or nuts. But you don't just have to stick with those – we've had a great time experimenting in the kitchen.

Meringue mixture is temperamental, so you need to work quickly. Be careful not to add too much flavouring, such as oily nuts or liquid, as it will deflate the mixture. We've come up with some winning flavours to try below, but feel free to experiment with your own – Willy Wonka style!

For all the flavours that follow we have used one batch of Meringue Girls Mixture.

CHOCOLATE:

Use **3 tbsp of good-quality 70% cocoa powder**. Fold a third (1 tbsp) into your meringue mixture until just combined before spooning the mixture into your piping bag. Once you have piped out all your chocolate kisses, dust the top of the meringues with the remaining cocoa.

HAZELNUT:

Use **3 tbsp of finely ground hazelnuts**. Fold a third (1 tbsp) into your meringue mixture and paint the inside of your piping bag with stripes of **natural amber food colouring**, before spooning the mixture into your piping bag. Once you have piped out all your hazelnut kisses, sprinkle with the remaining ground hazelnuts.

LAVENDER:

Fold **½ tsp of natural lavender essence** (or to taste) into your meringue mixture. Paint stripes in the inside of your piping bag with **natural purple and blue food colourings**, then spoon the mixture in before piping.

COCONUT:

Use **50g of dessicated coconut**. Fold half (25g) into your meringue mixture until just combined. Spoon the mixture into your piping bag, cut the tip and start piping. Once you have piped out all your coconut kisses, sprinkle the peaks with the remaining coconut.

PASSIONFRUIT:

Use **3 tsp of freeze-dried passion fruit powder**. Fold this into your meringue mixture then paint the inside of your piping bag with stripes of **natural yellow and purple food colouring**. Spoon the mixture in and start piping.

CINNAMON:

Use **1 tbsp of ground cinnamon**. Fold half (1/2 tbsp) into your meringue mixture then spoon the mixture into your piping bag. Once you have piped out all your cinnamon kisses, dust the top of the meringues with the remaining cinnamon, using a sieve.

HOT CROSS BUN:

Fold **1 tsp of mixed spice, 1 tsp of cinnamon and 1 tbsp of finely chopped mixed peel** into your meringue mixture. Paint the inside of your piping bag with stripes of **natural brown food colouring**, then spoon the mixture in and start piping. Try adding a 'cross' after baking using melted chocolate.

PISTACHIO AND ROSEWATER:

Use **50g of finely ground pistachios**. Fold a third (approx. 15g) into your meringue mixture along with **1 tsp of rosewater**. Paint the inside of your piping bag with stripes of **natural red food colouring**, then spoon in the mixture and start piping. Finish by sprinkling the meringues with the remaining finely ground pistachio.

GREEN TEA:

Fold **1 tbsp of Matcha green tea powder** into your meringue mixture. Paint the inside of your piping bag with stripes of **natural green food colouring**, then spoon the mixture in and start piping.

RASPBERRY:

Use **3 tbsp of freeze-dried raspberries ground into a fine powder**. Fold this into your meringue mixture and paint the inside of your piping bag with stripes of **natural pink food colouring**. Spoon the mixture in and start piping. Note: we've found that the freeze-dried raspberries burn if sprinkled on top.

GINGER:

Fold **2 tbsp of natural ground ginger** into your meringue mixture. Paint the inside of your piping bag with stripes of **natural orange food colouring**, then spoon the mixture in and pipe. Top with thin strips of stem or crystallized ginger if you fancy.

MANUKA HONEY:

Fold **3 tbsp of dried Manuka honey powder** into your meringue mixture. Paint the inside of your piping bag with stripes of **natural amber food colouring**, then spoon the mixture in and pipe.

STRAWBERRY AND BLACK PEPPER:

Use **3 tbsp of freeze-dried strawberries ground into a fine powder and ½ tsp of black pepper**. Fold this into your meringue mixture and paint the inside of your piping bag with stripes of **natural red food colouring**. Spoon the mixture into your piping bag and once you have piped out all your strawberry kisses, crack a tiny bit of black pepper over each meringue.

VANILLA POD:

Split lengthways and scrape out the **seeds from 1 whole vanilla pod** and fold into your meringue mixture, making sure the seeds are evenly dispersed. Spoon the mixture into your piping bag, cut the tip and start piping.

CHAI:

Use **1 tbsp of natural chai powder and 1 tsp of cardamom seeds** (break open the pods, discard the husk, and finely crush). Fold all the chai powder and half of the cardamom seeds (1/2 tsp) into your meringue mixture. Paint the inside of your piping bag with stripes of **natural amber food colouring**, then spoon the mixture in. Once you have piped out all of your chai kisses, sprinkle with the remaining crushed cardamom seeds.

The flavour possibilities are endless – just stick to the rules and get your creative juices flowing. Imagine Bounty (chocolate and coconut) or Ferrero Rocher (hazelnut and chocolate). Or try adding a tsp of strong natural essence: there are loads to try like white peach, yuzu, cranberry, apple, lemon or cherry.

When it comes to using flavoured kisses in puddings, they are very versatile, so you can pick and choose what flavour you use for the recipes that follow. Sometimes we've suggested the flavour if there is a clear winner.

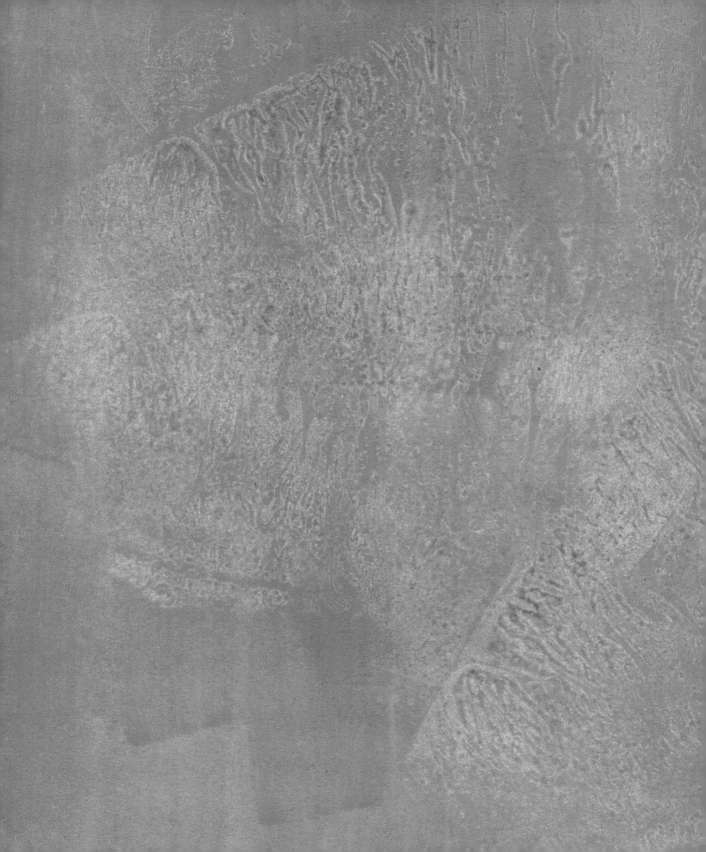

KISS
RECIPES

FILLINGS FOR KISSES

Sandwich your meringue kisses together with a variety of tasty fillings. Pop these on the table after dinner for the sweetest petits fours. Mix and match your kiss flavours with the filling flavours to create great taste sensations.

CHOCOLATE GANACHE:

Melt **50g of 70% dark chocolate** in a heatproof bowl set over a pan of simmering water (don't let the bowl come in contact with the water) or in a micro-safe bowl in the microwave on high for 1-2 minutes. Once melted, pour in **50ml of double cream**. Mix quickly with a spoon. The ganache should have a thick, smooth and silky consistency.

PEANUT BUTTER:

Mix **50g of crunchy peanut butter** with **2 tsp of icing sugar**. The filling should have a thick, nutty consistency and be just the right balance of salty and sweet.

LEMON AND POPPY SEED:

Mix **50g of Lemon Curd** (see recipe on p.140, or use good-quality shop-bought) with **½ tsp of poppy seeds and 30g of cream cheese**. This should have a thick, smooth and silky consistency and be a great balance of sour and sweet.

COFFEE CREAM:

Whisk **50g of double cream** to a stiff peak. Add **a small espresso shot** to the cream along with **1 tbsp of icing sugar**. The cream should have a thick, smooth and silky consistency.

NUTELLA BUTTERCREAM:

Whisk **50g of unsalted butter** at room temperature with **4 tbsp of Nutella** until very smooth, then whisk in **4 tbsp of icing sugar** and **a pinch of sea salt** until light and fluffy.

RAINBOW WEDDING TIER

This meringue wedding tier is a great alternative if you are bored with the standard wedding cake or cupcake tier and want your wedding to stand out from the rest. Make your kisses in batches and store for up to two weeks in an airtight container until you are ready to assemble your masterpiece.

FILLS A LARGE 7 LAYERED TIER

300 Meringue Kisses
 (see pp.30-35)

Make your Meringue Kisses in the colours and flavours of your choice (see pp.30-35). Remember that you will need more meringues for the larger bottom layer than the smallest top layer. On our tier, we have used approximately 8 coconut, 18 green tea, 25 yuzu, 37 ginger, 52 pistachio & rosewater, 70 raspberry and 90 chocolate.

FOR THE FULL RAINBOW EFFECT WE RECOMMEND TO ASSEMBLE IN THIS ORDER:

CHOCOLATE (BROWN)

RASPBERRY (PINK)

PISTACHIO AND ROSEWATER (RED)

GINGER (ORANGE)

YUZU (YELLOW)

GREEN TEA (GREEN)

COCONUT (WHITE)

But as with all our recipes, choose your colours and flavours to suit your mood.

KISS CANAPES WITH POMEGRANATE PROSECCO

Sometimes the simple things in life are best. Here we've paired up a meringue kiss with our favourite bubbly – heaven. This is perfect for a celebratory toast, or summer drinks with friends.

SERVES 8

35 Meringue Kisses
  (see pp.30–35)

FOR THE TOPPING:
100ml double cream
1 tbsp icing sugar
8 fresh raspberries

FOR THE POMEGRANATE PROSECCO:
1 bottle of Prosecco
200ml pomegranate juice
  (we use PomGreat)
Fresh pomegranate seeds

Make your Meringue Kisses in the flavour of your choice *(see pp.30–35)*.

To make the topping for your meringue kisses, pour the cream and icing sugar into a mixing bowl and whisk until just stiff, taking care not to over-whisk. Set aside.

Assemble your canapés by placing the meringue kisses on a beautiful serving platter. Dollop each kiss with 1 tsp of whipped cream and finish with a single fresh berry.

For the pomegranate Prosecco, pour 30ml of pomegranate juice into each champagne flute. Fill the rest of the flutes with Prosecco. Finish by dropping a few pomegranate seeds into each flute. Cheers!

MAYAN CHILLI HOT CHOCOLATE WITH FLOATING KISS

The Mayan chilli flavours give this hot chocolate a serious kick of winter warmth. Add a shot of Smoky Mezcal or Tequila to turn up the heat. The meringue kisses ooze and goo like marshmallows once they hit the hot chocolate.

SERVES 4

4 Chocolate Meringue Kisses
  (*see pp.30 & 32*)

FOR THE HOT CHOCOLATE:

1 red chilli
800ml full-fat milk
5 cardamom pods
5 cloves
2 cinnamon sticks
2 star anise
Handful of dark brown sugar,
  or to taste
1 tbsp good-quality
  dark cocoa powder
150g 70% dark chocolate
A splash of Mezcal or Tequila
  (optional – if you want to make
  it cheeky)

Make your Chocolate Kisses (*see pp.30 & 32*).

Slice the red chilli directly down the middle, retaining the seeds and all.

To infuse the milk, pour the milk into a medium-sized saucepan. Add the sliced chilli and the whole spices. Then add the brown sugar and cocoa powder. Place over a very low heat and slowly bring to a gentle simmer.

Once the spiced milk is simmering, take off the heat and strain through a sieve into another pan to get rid of the spices and the chilli. Place the milk back on a very low heat and add the dark chocolate. Stir until the chocolate has melted, then take off the heat. Taste to check if it needs more sugar.

Using your best teacups, pour your chocolate in while it's hot. Add a splash of booze, if using. Top with your beautiful meringue kisses.

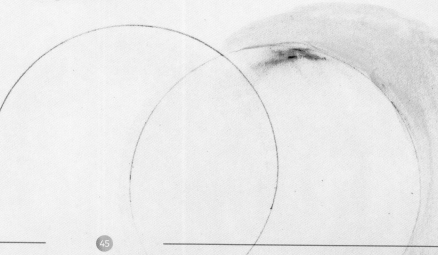

MERINGUE SURPRISES

A great one for a kid's party. Pipe your kisses over M&M's chocolates, or mini marshmallows for an amazing meringue surprise! If you want to get even more creative, try piping meringue kisses over whole hazelnuts, sour cherries, or even Revels (for a surprise within a surprise).

MAKES 35 KISSES

1 batch of uncooked Meringue Girls Mixture, flavoured with vanilla pod (see p.26 & 34)
1 small bag of baby marshmallows
1 small bag of M&M's

Preheat your oven to 100°C/gas ¼, and line a large baking sheet with baking paper.

Make your meringue mixture and flavour it with vanilla pod (see pp.26 & 34).

Place 35 'surprises' (mini marshmallows and M&M's) in total on the baking sheet, leaving a 2cm space around each surprise.

Pipe a vanilla pod kiss directly on top of each little surprise.

Bake for 30-40 minutes, or until the bases of the meringues lift off the sheet with ease.

These will keep for 2 weeks, covered with cling film or placed in an airtight container and stored in a cool, dry place.

BEETROOT AND CHOCOLATE
BARBIE CAKE

SERVES 12

1 batch of uncooked Meringue
Girls Mixture, divided into
6 colours of your choice
(*see pp.26-31*)

FOR THE CAKE:

350g plain flour
20g baking powder
150g good-quality
   dark cocoa powder
450g caster sugar
6 free-range eggs
450g cooked beetroot
400ml vegetable oil

FOR THE CREAM CHEESE ICING:

400g cream cheese
100g double cream
4 tbsp of icing sugar

EXTRAS:

1 Barbie doll (clothes and legs
   removed) or doll pick
Beads and Barbie accessories

We have a little confession to make – we have an obsession
with Barbie cakes. This is the perfect cake for a kid's party
– or a big kid's party – and we've stuck miniature meringue
kisses around the skirt for extra bling bling.

This beetroot and chocolate recipe is so simple to make
and always produces a rich chocolately and moist cake.
The best thing about a Barbie cake is that you can be so
creative. Who do you wanna be – Malibu Barbie, Disco
Barbie or Meringue Girl Barbie?

Preheat your oven to 100°C/gas ¼ and line a large baking
sheet with baking paper.

Make your meringue mixture, divide it into 6 portions and
then colour and flavour them to your liking. Use the method
described on p.32, but cut the tip off the piping bag to the
size on a 5p coin. These mini kisses will bake in half the time
that normal kisses take, so put them in the oven for about
20 minutes, or until they lift off the baking paper with their
bases intact.

Once your meringues are done, turn the oven up to 180°C/gas 4.
Grease and line a 20cm cake tin (preferably a springform tin),
and grease and line a deep 20cm rimmed aluminium bowl.

Sift the flour, baking powder, cocoa and sugar into a bowl.
Blend the eggs, beetroot and oil in a blender until smooth,
then fold the beetroot mixture into the dry ingredients.

Pour half the mixture into your prepared cake tin and the rest into your lined aluminium bowl. Bake for 40 minutes.

Meanwhile, bling out your Barbie – anything from goth to glam, it's up to you.

Remove the cakes from the oven and leave to cool in their tin and bowl.

For the cream cheese icing, whisk double cream into stiff peaks, then whisk in the cream cheese and icing sugar until smooth and stiff.

Once the cakes have cooled, remove them from their tin and bowl, and cool on a wire rack.

Spread the springform-tin cake with a layer of cream cheese icing, reserving the remainder. Turn the aluminium-bowl cake upside down and place on top of the cream cheese. Shave the cake with a knife to mould it into the perfect skirt shape.

Use a long knife (such as a bread knife) to cut a hole in the centre of the cake, deep enough for Barbie's hips to fit into, up to just below her waist. Generously cover the cake with the remaining cream cheese icing, taking care to work around Barbie's waist.

Lastly, gently place the meringue kisses, layer by layer, on the cake, starting from Barbie's waist and working down, alternating the colours to form a beautiful, colourful meringue kiss skirt.

MERINGUE PROFITEROLES

Meringue kisses filled with cream – this is by far the most delicious way to use up leftover meringue kisses. This works best when the kisses have dried out for a few days after baking as they will have a harder shell. Although it's great to use up leftovers, it's worth making a batch of kisses in advance just to try this one out.

MAKES 35

35 1-2-week-old Meringue Kisses
  (see pp.30-35)

FOR THE FILLING:
200g Double cream
1 tsp Icing sugar
30g Lemon Curd (see p.140)
  or 30g raspberry coulis, to
  flavour the cream (optional)

FOR THE COULIS:
30g frozen raspberries
½ tsp honey
1 tsp water

Make your Meringue Kisses in advance (see pp.30-35).

Use a small sharp knife to make a small hole in the base of each meringue kiss – just big enough for a very small piping nozzle to fit in it.

Whisk the double cream and icing sugar until the mixture just holds its shape (it tends to whisk further in the piping bag). If you want, you can add lemon curd or coulis to flavour the cream.

To make the coulis tip all of the ingredients into a saucepan and bring to the boil. Turn heat down and simmer gently for a further 5 minutes. Whiz in a food processor until smooth and set aside to cool.

Spoon the cream into a disposable piping bag fitted with a very small nozzle (sometimes we use a plastic syringe).

Pipe the cream into the holes, aiming to fill with as much cream as possible.

Eat on their own, or assemble them into a profiterole tower.

Eat quickly.

FERRERO ROCHER MERINGUE TOWER

Ambassador, with this tower you are really spoiling us. A quirky play on the iconic Ferrero Rocher celebration tower – and a sign of good taste!

---

35 Hazelnut Kisses (see pp.30 & 32)

FOR THE WHIPPED CREAM:
250ml double cream
1 tbsp icing sugar

FOR THE GANACHE:
200g 70% dark chocolate
200g double cream

EXTRAS:
Ferrero Rochers
Toasted hazelnuts
Edible gold leaf

Make your Hazelnut Kisses (see pp.30 & 32).

Prepare the whipped cream. With a hand whisk, whisk the icing sugar and double cream until just stiff, taking care not to over-whisk. Set aside.

To make the chocolate ganache, break the chocolate into pieces and put into a heatproof mixing bowl set over a pan of simmering water, or put the chocolate in a micro-safe bowl and melt it in the microwave for 1-2 minutes on high, taking care not to let the chocolate burn. Once the chocolate has melted, fold in the double cream until just mixed. The ganache should be thick and silky.

Get out a beautiful gold serving platter. Start by sticking down the bottom triangle layer of kisses with ganache to the platter. Then build up your tower layer by layer using cream and ganache as your tasty cement.

Once you have built your chocolatey, hazelnuty, creamy, meringue pyramid, fill in all the gaps and decorate with toasted hazelnuts, Ferrero Rochers and finish with edible gold leaf.

Summery
Desserts

LOVE HEARTS WITH RHUBARB AND STEM GINGER

A seriously cute and delicious dessert, this is ideal for Valentine's Day or a special occasion.

MAKES 6-8 MEDIUM HEARTS

---

1 batch of uncooked Meringue Girls Mixture (see p.26)

FOR THE WHIPPED CREAM:
250ml double cream
1½ tbsp icing sugar

TO DECORATE:
2-3 stems of fresh rhubarb
2-3 balls of stem ginger
A tbsp of icing sugar
A tbsp of caster sugar

Make your meringue mixture (see p.26).

Preheat your oven to 100°C/gas ¼, and line 2 baking sheets with baking paper. Fill a piping bag with your meringue mixture and cut a 20p-sized hole in the tip, then dollop the corners of the baking paper with some mixture and use like glue to stick the paper to the baking sheet.

Start by piping a medium heart shape, and then flll in the middle with more meringue mixture. Build up the walls of the heart by piping around the outside 2 more times. For a smoother, more natural shape, use a damp finger to smooth the base and edges before baking. Continue to pipe the rest of the hearts.

Bake for 45 minutes or until the meringues lift off the baking paper with their bases intact. If the hearts still have gooey bases, turn the oven off and leave in the oven to cool for another 15 minutes.

Once cooked, leave to cool. If you're not ready to serve them, store in an airtight container for up to 2 weeks.

When you are ready to serve, preheat the oven to 180c, then chop the rhubarb into small fingers, place in a small roasting tray and sprinkle with 1 tbsp of caster sugar. Bake for 6-8 minutes, or until the rhubarb pieces are soft but still holding their shape. Chop the stem ginger into neat slithers, then whip the double cream with some icing sugar until it holds soft peaks. Decorate with the pink rhubarb and fiery stem ginger.

STRAWBERRY MERINGUE ICE LOLLIES

A fabulous treat to pull out of the freezer on a hot summer's day. Fresh strawberry and crushed meringue ice lollies will put a smile on everyone's face. So simple and quick to make.

MAKES 6 LOLLIES

6 Meringue Kisses to crumble (*see pp.30-35*), or pieces of older broken meringues
50g caster sugar
60ml water
250 strawberries, stalks removed, cut in half
Juice of 1 orange
Popping candy, to serve (optional)

Make the Meringue Kisses (*see pp.30-35*), or use leftover pieces of broken meringue.

Pour the sugar and water into a heavy-bottomed pan and boil for 5 minutes until syrupy. Leave to cool.

Mash up the strawberries really well with a fork or in a food processor. Add the strawberry purée to the sugar syrup and pour in the orange juice.

Take 6 ice lolly moulds. Fill a quarter of each mould with juice, then crumble in the meringue pieces. Continue to add juice and crushed meringue until each mould is full. Freeze until solid. If there is any left over mixture, fill up an ice cube tray.

For an extra treat, dip the ice lollies in popping candy before eating – the kids will go wild.

RASPBERRY RIPPLE MERINGUE GELATO

A great way of using up leftover meringues that have lost their middle gooeyness, or if some didn't turn out as prettily as you would have hoped. This a no fuss, no-churn ice cream that you can simply freeze and then scoop into portions when you're ready to serve.

SERVES 8

350g raspberries,
  plus extra for serving
3 free-range medium eggs
100g golden caster sugar
300ml double cream
Leftover broken meringue bits
  (the more the better)
Melted dark chocolate to serve
  (optional)

With a fork, mash 150g of the raspberries, or whiz in a food processor until very smooth. Set aside.

Line a 1 litre loaf tin with cling film, overlapping the layers and leaving a large enough overhang so you can easily remove the frozen ice cream later.

In a heatproof bowl set over a pan of simmering water, whisk the eggs and sugar continuously with an electric whisk, until the mixture has doubled in volume. It will take about 10 minutes to get it really thick.

Remove from the heat, then continue to whisk until the mixture is completely cool. Now whisk the cream until it's thick and just holding its shape. Fold the egg mix into the cream, then carefully fold in the crumbled pieces of meringue.

Pour some of the raspberry purée into the bottom of the loaf tin, then gently add the cream mixture and use the rest of the raspberry purée to ripple through. Freeze for at least 5 hours, or ideally overnight.

When ready to serve, remove from the freezer and allow it to soften slightly, then use the cling film to pull it out of the loaf tin. You can either cut into slices of scoop into balls. Drizzle with melted dark chocolate if you fancy a further flourish.

LEMON MERINGUE CAKE

This cake has a little secret: it's filled with delicious lemon curd, which oozes out when a slice is cut. It is an extremely tangy and moist cake. We use our Marshmallow Meringue recipe on p.148, to give a wonderfully gooey frosting that holds its shape.

SERVES 8

FOR THE CAKE MIX:
225g butter
225g caster sugar
4 medium eggs
2 tsp vanilla extract
150g self-raising flour
75g ground almonds
A little milk
Zest and juice of 2 unwaxed lemons

FOR THE TOPPING:
1/2 batch of uncooked Marshmallow
   Meringue mixture (*see p.148*)

FOR THE FILLING:
400g Lemon Curd (*see p.140*),
   or use good quality shop bought

Preheat the oven to 180°C/gas 4. Grease and line a 1 litre loaf tin with baking paper.

To prepare the cake batter, cream the butter and the sugar together in a bowl until pale and fluffy. Beat in the eggs, a little at a time, and stir in the vanilla extract. Fold in the flour, using a large metal spoon, adding a little extra milk if necessary to create a batter with a soft dropping consistency. Spoon the mixture into the loaf tin and gently even it out with a spatula.

Bake the cake for 20-25 minutes, or until golden brown on top and a skewer inserted into the middle comes out clean.

Remove from the oven and set aside to rest for 5 minutes, then remove from the tin and peel off the paper. Place on a wire cooling rack to cool completely.

While the cake is cooling, make your Marshmallow Meringue mixture (*see p.148*).

Once the cake has cooled, scoop out a hole in the middle of the cake and fill with the lemon curd. The removed cake middle isn't needed for this recipe, so is the baker's treat!

Finish the cake by icing with the marshmallow meringue mixture. This cake will keep for 3 days in an airtight container in the fridge.

'MIX AND MATCH' SUMMERY ETON MESS

An exciting twist on a British summertime favourite. Mix and match your meringue kisses to create a delicious seasonal Eton mess. Well, actually not that messy... rather beautiful, we think.

SERVES 6–8

35 Meringue Kisses (*see pp.30-35*)

FOR THE COULIS:
250g frozen raspberries
1 tbsp honey

FOR THE WHIPPED CREAM:
500ml double cream
2 tbsp icing sugar

FOR THE TOPPING:
400g fresh seasonal berries
  (raspberries, blueberries or
  strawberries or a mixture)
2 tbsp freeze-dried raspberries

Make your Meringue Kisses (*see pp.30-35*).

To make the coulis, place the frozen raspberries into a small saucepan, drizzle the honey over them and place over a medium heat. Once the coulis is bubbling, turn the heat down to a gentle simmer and continue cooking for another 10 minutes. Once the coulis has cooled a little, taste and adjust the sweetness if necessary. You want it to be quite tart as the meringues are very sweet. Whiz the coulis with a hand blender until smooth and then set aside to cool completely.

For the whipped cream, pour the double cream and icing sugar into a mixing bowl and whisk to a medium-thick consistency, taking care not to over-whisk.

When you are 10 minutes away from serving your Eton mess – and only then – start to assemble everything. If you do this too early, you'll end up with a soggy mess.

Arrange the Meringue Kisses on a serving platter. Dollop the cream all around the meringues and place the berries on top of the cream. Lather with your freshly made coulis and then, to finish, sprinkle the freeze-dried raspberries over everything. Be as creative as you like by adding nuts or drizzled chocolate if you want.

POMEGRANATE
MERINGUE TRAY BAKE

Ruby red pomegranate seeds, crème fraîche, green pistachio slivers and a quick and easy mint sugar. This Middle Eastern-inspired tray bake looks and tastes the business.

1 batch of uncooked Meringue Girls Mixture *(see p.26)*
½ tsp of natural pink food colouring
1 small bunch of fresh mint
50g of caster sugar
600g of crème fraîche
100g of fresh pomegranate seeds, or 1 whole pomegranate
100g of pistachios (as green as you can find)
50g of pomegranate molasses

Preheat the oven to 100°C/gas ¼.

Make your meringue mixture *(see p.26)*. Put a blob of the mixture on each corner of a small baking sheet, then line the sheet with baking paper and use the meringue like glue to stick the paper down.

Use the back of a large spoon to spread the remaining mixture into a rough A4 rectangle on the baking paper. Swirl the pink natural food colouring through the mixture, using the tip of a knife, to marble the meringue.

Bake for 1 hour, or until the meringue is crisp on the outside and easily lifts off the paper with its base intact. Leave to cool on the tray.

Whiz the fresh mint and caster sugar in a food processor, or use a pestle and mortar to crush the mint and sugar.

When ready to serve, dollop the meringue with crème fraîche, fresh pomegranate seeds, green pistachios and the mint sugar. To finish, drizzle with pomegranate molasses.

LEMON SORBET MERINGUE CRUNCH

This is another tasty way of using up broken or dried-out meringues. You can make your own sorbet, but shop-bought is fine. This makes a lovely summer party treat. The sweet, crushed meringue balances out the tangy lemon sorbet and gives a brilliant texture for a lemon meringue – a match made in heaven.

SERVES 4–6

About 10 1-2-week-old Meringue Kisses (*see pp.30-35*)
Waffle ice cream cones, to serve

FOR THE LEMON SORBET:
500g caster sugar
750ml water
250ml lemon juice
(from 6–8 lemons)
Zest of 1 unwaxed lemon

Make your Meringue Kisses in advance (*see pp.30-35*).

To make the sorbet, pour the sugar and water into a heavy-bottomed pan. Heat gently until the sugar dissolves, then simmer for a couple of minutes. Stir in the lemon juice and zest and leave to cool.

Churn the liquid in an ice cream machine. Alternatively, pour into a tub, place in the freezer and beat with a fork every 30 minutes until you have a smooth texture.

While the sorbet is freezing, crush the meringues into fine crumbs and scatter onto a flat tray. Once the lemon mixture has reached sorbet consistency, start scooping balls of sorbet and cover with meringue crumbs by rolling them around the flat tray. Work quickly so the sorbet does not melt.

Serve immediately in cones.

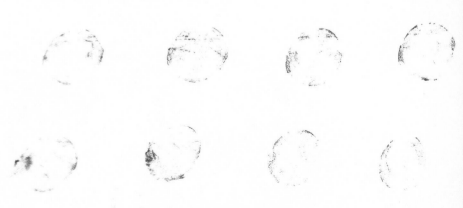

PISTACHIO AND ROSEWATER PAVLOVA WITH GREEK YOGHURT, HONEY AND FIGS

A Middle Eastern-inspired pavlova, which uses Greek yoghurt instead of cream. It's a stunning, fresh dessert filled with figs, green pistachio and topped with runny honey and rose petals.

SERVES 6–8

1 batch of uncooked Meringue
  Girls Mixture (*see p.26*)
100g green pistachios
1 tbsp rosewater
8 figs
300g thick Greek yoghurt
4 tbsp runny honey
Fresh rose petals, to decorate

Preheat your oven to 100°C/gas ¼, and line a small baking sheet with baking paper.

Make your meringue mixture (*see p.26*).

Finely grind half of the pistachios and add half of this to your stiff, uncooked meringue mixture along with the rosewater. Fold gently to incorporate all the ingredients but be very careful not to knock out any of the volume.

Working quickly, spoon the flavoured meringue mixture onto the centre of the baking sheet and mould into the shape of a 10 inch spiky circle with your spoon. Then use the back of the spoon to make a slight dip in the centre of the meringue to form a large well.

Sprinkle with the rest of the finely ground pistachios and bake for about 2 hours. When cooked, the large meringue nest should have a firm base and easily come away from the baking paper. Set aside to cool.

Slice the figs into quarters and roughly chop the remaining pistachios. Now you are ready to plate up.

Place the cooled pavlova in the centre of a serving platter. Spoon the Greek yoghurt into the groove of the meringue nest and have some oozing down the sides. Place most of the figs on top of the yoghurt and a scatter a few around the plate. Lather the whole masterpiece with honey. Finish by scattering the roughly chopped pistachios and fresh rose petals over the top.

MERINGUE RAINBOW CAKE

SERVES 12

2 batches of uncooked Meringue
   Girls Mixture (*see p.26*)
Wilton's Gels food colouring
   (red, orange, yellow, green,
   blue and purple)
Seeds scraped from 2 vanilla pods
500ml double cream
Smarties, to decorate (optional)

The mother of all rainbow cakes, this epic bright meringue layer cake takes a bit of work, but is worth it.

We've suggested making this in 2 batches so that it fits in the oven. Make a batch of meringue mixture at a time. Use the first batch to make red, orange and yellow discs, and the second batch to make green, blue and purple discs.

To achieve a real popping colour, we advocate using man-made food dyes (Wilton's Gels work really well). The trick to bright disc edges is to cover the inside of each piping bag halfway up with each disc colour. If you just colour the mixture without piping you won't get the vibrant colour but you will still get a nice pastel shade.

We've flavoured the discs with vanilla seeds, but you can choose any of our kisses flavourings (*see p.32-35*).

Preheat your oven to 100°C/gas ¼, and line 3 baking sheets with baking paper.

Make your first batch of meringue mixture (*see p.26*), and fold through the seeds of one of your vanilla pods, and then thickly paint the inside of three piping bags with your first three rainbow colours – red, orange and yellow. Fill the piping bags evenly and then pipe a 10 inch circle on each baking sheet, starting from the outside of the circle and snailing inwards to the very centre.

When you have finished, gently smooth the top of the discs to get rid of the swirly effect, until you have beautiful flat 1-inch thick discs. While the first discs are cooking, repeat the process to make green, blue and purple discs.

Bake for 1 hour, or until the meringue discs easily lift off the baking paper with their bases intact. Leave to cool on the baking sheets.

Keep all discs in an airtight container or carefully wrapped in cling film for up to 2 weeks, until you are ready to use.

When ready to serve, whisk the double cream until it just holds its peaks. Stack the meringue discs on a cake stand, alternating the colours and spreading layers of whipped cream in between each one. Decorate with Smarties if you're feeling extra colourful.

GRILLED PEACHES FILLED AND CRUSHED AMARETTO BISCUITS WITH MAPLE MERINGUE

This uses maple syrup instead of sugar syrup as in a traditional Italian Meringue *(see p.150)*. Just heat the maple syrup to a high temperature and add it to the stiffened egg whites.

The Maple Meringue mixture is delicious both baked and unbaked, with a lovely maple flavour and golden colour. It can be used as a substitute in most recipes in this book. Here, we've used unbaked meringue, lightly toasted, dolloped on top of grilled peaches filled with amaretto biscuits. For a summery dessert – try grilling the peaches on a barbecue.

SERVES 4

4 peaches, halved with
  stones removed
Amaretto biscuits, crumbled
½ batch of uncooked Maple
  Meringue mixture *(see p.152)*

Start by making ½ a batch of Maple Meringue mixture *(see page 152)*.

Preheat oven to 180c, then fry the peaches, cut-side down, on a hot griddle pan until they have blackened lines and are softening. Place in the oven until softened.

Fill the griddled peaches with crushed amaretto biscuits, and dollop Maple Meringue on top. To finish, blow-torch the meringue or flash under a hot grill until golden.

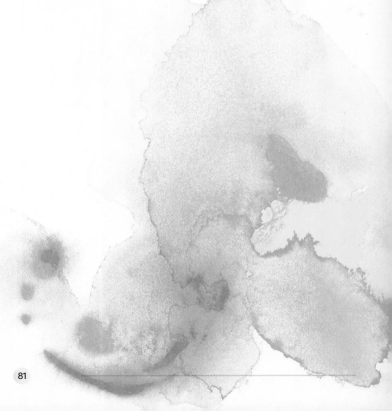

LEMONGRASS AND CHILLI MERINGUE PIE

SERVES 8

FOR THE SWEET SHORTCRUST PASTRY:

225g plain flour
25g icing sugar
Pinch of salt
150g chilled butter, cut into cubes
1 egg yolk
3 tbsp iced water
A little beaten egg and water,
   for the egg wash

FOR THE FILLING AND TOPPING:

600g of Lemongrass and Chilli
   Curd (see p.140), or use good-
   quality shop-bought lemon
   curd and add 1 tsp of
   lemongrass paste and a pinch
   of chilli flakes
½ batch of uncooked Italian
   Meringue mixture (see p.150)

This zingy variation on the classic lemon meringue pie includes a touch of lemongrass. You can easily adapt the recipe to make any citrus meringue pie – try it with pink grapefruits, limes, Seville oranges or blood oranges, using 400ml of freshly squeezed juice. You can make your own sweet shortcrust pastry or buy ready-made.

Preheat the oven to 200°C/gas 6.

For the pastry, sift the flour, sugar and salt into a large bowl and then, using your fingertips, rub in the butter until the mixture resembles breadcrumbs.

Mix the egg yolk with the cold water.

Using a knife, stir the yolky water through the flour and butter mixture until you have a dough. Knead quickly and gently until smooth, then shape into a flat disc, wrap in cling film and chill for 30 minutes. (You can use a food processor, but be careful not to over-process the dough and make it chewy.)

On a lightly floured work surface, roll out the pastry and then line a 25cm loose-bottomed tart tin with the pastry, letting any excess hang over the sides. Prick the pastry lightly with a fork, then line with baking paper, fill with rice or baking beans to weight the paper down and place on a baking sheet.

Bake the pastry 'blind' for 12 minutes. Then remove and discard the baking paper, brush the bottom of the tart with the egg wash and return to the oven for another 8–10 minutes until the pastry is cooked and slightly golden. Turn the oven down to 180c.

Make the Lemongrass and Chilli Curd (*see p.140*) or use shop-bought. Fill your cooked tart base and bake for 15 minutes until the curd is set. Allow to cool in the tin on a wire rack.

Make your Italian Meringue (*see p.150*).

Spoon the stiff meringue over the top, starting in the middle and swirling into peaks.

Flash under a hot grill or toast the tips until golden with a blowtorch.

ALMOND MERINGUE ROULADE

This recipe uses just three core ingredients to make a deliciously light and airy almond cake which is gluten free. We have rolled it into a roulade with fresh cream and raspberries.

SERVES 8

6 free-range eggs, separated
200g caster sugar
200g ground almonds
Butter, for greasing cake tin

TO SERVE:
100g whipped cream
50g toasted almonds
50g fresh raspberries,
  roughly mashed with a fork
Icing sugar, to dust
Extra fresh raspberries to serve

Preheat the oven to 170°C/gas 3. Lightly grease and line a swiss roll tin or shallow baking tray.

Using an electric whisk, whisk the 6 yolks and the caster sugar together until very thick and pale. Gently fold in the ground almonds.

In a clean bowl, whisk the 6 egg whites until stiff. Then gently fold them into the yolk mixture until just combined.

Carefully pour the batter into the swiss roll tin and bake for 25 minutes, until the cake begins to come away from the sides of the tin and a skewer inserted into the middle of the cake comes out clean.

Leave the cake to cool in the tin for 15 minutes, then take it out of the tin and let it cool completely on a wire cooling rack. Keep the baking paper attached, to the cake, as it will help your to roll the roulade.

When you are ready to serve, spread the whole of the roulade with a thin layer of whipped cream, then spread over the mashed raspberries.

To roll the roulade, use the baking paper to help you to tightly roll the cake from one end to another. Sprinkle the top with toasted flaked almonds and dust with icing sugar. Serve with more fresh raspberries.

GOOSEBERRY AND STRAWBERRY MERINGUE COMPOTE JARS

Tangy, fresh and light Gooseberry & Strawberry Compote Jars are topped with golden meringue. These are a low-fat but delicious dessert to finish off a meal on a summer's day.

MAKES 4

FOR THE COMPOTE:
400g of whole strawberries, hulled (frozen is fine)
100g gooseberries, topped and tailed
2 tbs honey

TO FINISH:
100g strawberries hulled and quartered
½ Meringue Girls Mixture

4 x 150g jam jars, or small glass bowls

Start by making the compote. Add the whole hulled strawberries and topped-and-tailed gooseberries into a saucepan and place over a medium heat. Drizzle over the honey and cook gently for 7-10 minutes until the fruit is soft but still holding its shape. The compote should be chunky and a little bit tangy.

Now you are ready to fill the jars.

Fill the jam jars 1/3 of the way with your compote, then top with quartered strawberries until your jars are 2/3 full. Pipe or spoon in the meringue mixture to fill the jars to the brim. Blowtorch or flash under a hot grill until the tops are golden.

These can be prepared a couple of hours in advance and kept in the fridge, but it is best to blowtorch or grill the tops at the very last minute.

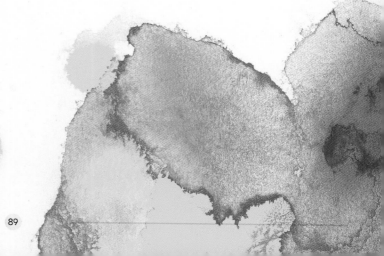

LEMON MERINGUE WAFFLES

Hot waffles sandwiched with tangy lemon curd and fluffy meringue – decadently delicious. You can make your own waffles, or you can buy shop bought waffles and heat them up in a toaster.

SERVES 4

FOR THE WAFFLES:

250g plain flour
1 ½ tsp baking powder
2 tbsp caster sugar
1 tsp salt
2 eggs
475ml milk
30ml vegetable oil,
  plus extra for waffle maker
Icing sugar, for dusting

TO SERVE:

150g of Lemon Curd (see p.140),
  or use good-quality shop-bought
½ batch of Italian Meringue
  (see p.150)

To make the waffles, place all the dry ingredients in a large mixing bowl. In a separate bowl, beat together the eggs and milk, then add to the dry ingredients. Add the vegetable oil and mix all the ingredients together until all the large lumps have been broken up. Do not overmix or the waffles will be heavy when cooked.

Preheat the waffle maker and brush with oil.

Pour three quarters of a cup of batter into the waffle maker and cook for 3-4 minutes, or until golden brown and crispy on the outside. Repeat with the remaining batter until you have enough waffles.

To serve, spread 1 hot waffle with tangy lemon curd and another with mallowy meringue. Sandwich together and dust with some icing sugar. Serve as a stack, and demolish!

Unused waffle batter will keep in the fridge for up to 2 days.

wintery puddings

COOKIE DOUGH MERINGUE SLICE

A chocolate chip chewy cookie dough base, topped with baked golden caster sugar meringue. So moreish.

MAKES 12 SMALL SLICES

FOR THE COOKIE DOUGH BASE:

250g plain flour

½ tsp bicarbonate of soda

½ tsp salt

170g unsalted butter, melted, plus extra for greasing tin

100g golden caster sugar

1 tbsp vanilla extract

1 egg

1 egg yolk

325g chocolate chips

FOR THE MERINGUE:

120g free-range egg whites (4 medium eggs)

240g golden caster sugar

Preheat the oven to 180°C/gas 4. Cut 2 pieces of baking paper and line a shallow A4 baking tray so that there is some overhang for easy removal once the meringue has cooled. Lightly grease with butter.

Make the cookie dough. In a bowl, sift together the flour, bicarbonate of soda and salt. In a separate medium bowl, cream together the melted butter, brown sugar and caster sugar until well blended. Beat in the vanilla, egg and egg yolk until light and creamy. Then mix in the sifted ingredients until just blended and crumbly.

Press the cookie dough gently into the base of the baking tray with your hands, making sure the surface is even. Sprinkle the chocolate chips on top of the cookie dough and press them down lightly. Bake the base for 15 minutes until just cooked but still soft, it will harden further when it cools.

Turn the oven up to 200c. Using the Meringue Girls Mixture method (*page 26*), heat the golden caster sugar at 200c until the edges caramelize and whisk into the stiff egg whites to make a stiff and glossy meringue. Use a spatula to spread meringue on top of the cookie base, starting from the middle to the edges.

Lightly press a piece of baking paper over the top of the meringue. Turn the oven down to 180c and bake for another 10 minutes, then remove the baking paper and bake for another 5 minutes until the meringue peaks are golden.

Leave to cool completely before cutting into 12 slices.

HONEYCOMB, CHOCOLATE AND SALTED PEANUT MERINGUES

Big, spiky and chewy chocolate meringues rolled in honeycomb, cocoa and salted peanuts. These sweet and slightly salty meringues are delicious eaten just as they are. To take them over the edge, drizzle with melted milk chocolate and serve with a big dollop of thick Greek yoghurt.

MAKES 6 BIG ONES

1 batch of uncooked Meringue
  Girls Mixture (*see p.26*)
1 Crunchie bar or a small block
  of honeycomb, crumbled
8 tbsp good-quality dark
  cocoa powder
50g salted peanuts,
  roughly chopped

Line a large baking sheet with baking paper, and preheat the oven to 100°C/gas ¼.

Make the meringue mixture (*see p.26*), then carefully fold through half of the crumbled honeycomb and 1 tbsp of the cocoa powder.

Scatter the chopped peanuts and the rest of the cocoa powder and crumbled honeycomb over a large plate or baking tray.

Using 2 large metal spoons, take a big dollop of the stiff meringue mixture and roll it over the peanuts, cocoa powder and honeycomb so it sticks to the meringue and forms a lovely crunchy coating. Repeat with the remaining meringue mixture.

Place the meringues on the lined baking tray, leaving enough space between them so they have room to expand. Bake for 2 hours, or until they easily lift off the baking paper with their bases intact.

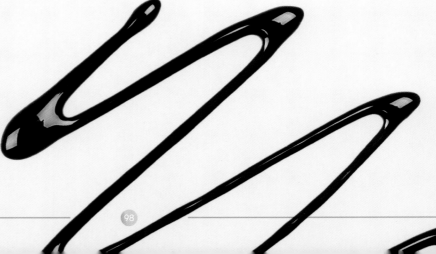

FROZEN BERRIES AND HOT CUSTARD WITH MADAGASCAN VANILLA POD MERINGUE

Such a simple but effective combination using frozen berries, home-made or shop-bought custard and leftover meringues. The hot custard thaws the berries and melts the meringues ever so slightly. An explosion on the senses – hot, cold, fresh and crunchy.

SERVES 8

16 Vanilla Pod Meringue Kisses
   (see pp.30 & 34)
1 batch of hot Vanilla Custard
   (see p.143), or use good-quality
   shop-bought
250g frozen berries

Make your Vanilla Pod Kisses in advance (see p.30 & 34), or use leftover meringues.

Make your custard, following the recipe on p.143 (or heat up your shop-bought custard). Once this is in a pouring jug, you are ready to serve.

Fill small individual serving bowls with frozen berries and Vanilla Pod Meringue Kisses. When at the dining table, allow your guests to drizzle over the steaming hot custard, and eat as the berries thaw.

PRETZEL CHOCOLATE
MARSHMALLOW MERINGUE TART

A no-bake, salty biscuit base, topped with rich chocolate and chewy Marshmallow Meringue. Everyone asks us for this recipe.

SERVES 6-8

FOR THE PRETZEL BASE:
100g salted pretzels
100g digestive biscuits
100g butter, plus a touch extra
  for greasing tin
50g golden syrup

FOR THE CHOCOLATE FILLING:
500g of double cream
400g of 70% dark bitter chocolate
Large pinch of Maldon sea salt

FOR THE TOPPING:
½ batch Meringue Girls Mixture
  (see p.26)
10 big marshmallows

Brush a 20cm loose-bottomed tart tin with a little melted butter.

Blitz the pretzels and digestives in a food processor or place in a plastic bag and bash with a rolling pin. Tip the pretzel and biscuit crumbs into a bowl.

Melt the butter and golden syrup together and then pour over the biscuit base and mix well. Using the back of a spoon, firmly press the base into your prepared tart tin, then chill in the fridge to set.

Break the chocolate into pieces and put into a heatproof mixing bowl set over a pan of simmering water, or put the chocolate in a micro-safe bowl and melt it in the microwave for 1-2 minutes on high. Add in the double cream and sea salt and stir until smooth and thick. Pour this chocolate ganache on top of the pretzel tart whilst still in the tin. Chill for at least 2 hours, or up to 2 days.

Make ½ a batch of Meringue Girls Mixture (see p.26), then melt the marshmallows in a heatproof mixing bowl set over a pan of simmering water, or in a micro-safe bowl and melt it in the microwave for 1-2 minutes on high. Stir the melted marshallow into the stiff meringue mixture.

Dollop the Marshmallow Meringue over the ganache and chill in the fridge until set. The gelatine in the marshmallows will set the meringue, so there is no need to bake. It also gives a really gooey texture. Flash it under a hot grill for a few minutes. Cut into nice clean slices with a knife dipped in hot water.

MINI PASSION FRUIT FILO MERINGUE PIES

Everyone will go will go crazy for these Mini Passion Fruit Meringue Pies. Filo pastry is a lower fat, light and easy alternative to shortcrust pastry.

MAKES 8

8 large sheets of filo pastry
100g melted butter, or oil spray
½ batch of uncooked Italian Meringue mixture *(see p.150)*
300g Passion Fruit Curd *(see p.139)*, or use good-quality shop-bought
2 whole passion fruits, pulp and pips scooped out for garnish

Preheat the oven to 180°C/gas 4. Grease a 12-hole mini mini muffin tin with a little butter or oil spray.

Cut the filo sheets into quarters to make 32 filo squares. Working quickly so the pastry doesn't dry out, place 1 sheet of filo at a time into the muffin holes and, using a pastry brush, coat each square with the melted butter, or spritz with oil spray.

Build up to 4 layers of filo per cup, overlapping the layers and forming a fan shape, continuing to brush between the layers with butter or oil spray so that when baked, the filo cup goes crispy.

Bake the shells for 7 minutes until lightly golden. Once the shells are out of the oven, spoon in the curd until each shell is three quarters full.

Place back in the oven and bake for another 5 minutes until the curd is set and the edges are golden brown. Remove from the oven and set aside.

Pipe or dollop about 1 tbsp of meringue mixture on top of each individual curd-filled filo case.

Either use a blowtorch to brown the meringue peaks or place back in the oven until golden. To finish, drizzle passion fruit pulp over the top of each case.

SALTED CARAMEL, POACHED PEAR AND CHOCOLATE DRIZZLE TRAY BAKE

SERVES 8

1 batch of uncooked Meringue
   Girls Mixture (*see p.26*)
2 tbsp good-quality dark
   cocoa powder
4 firm but ripe pears
1 small tin of dulce de leche
   or Carnation caramel sauce
A large pinch of Maldon sea salt
1 large tub of mascarpone
100g walnuts halves, toasted
100g 70% dark chocolate, melted,
   for drizzling

FOR THE PEAR POACHING LIQUID:

1 litre water
5 tbsp granulated sugar
1 cinnamon stick

Oozy dulche de leche, poached pears, drizzled chocolate, mascarpone and walnuts – an autumnal dessert dream. This easy and impressive tray bake is perfect for a casual dinner party where everyone can just get stuck in. Simply spread the uncooked meringue mixture over a lined baking tray and cook for 1 hour. Then swirl and drizzle on the toppings in Jackson Pollock style.

To save time, you can use tinned pears, but they won't have the amazing flavour and texture that these will have.

Make your meringue mixture (*see p.26*).

Preheat your oven to 100°C/gas ¼, and line a small baking sheet with baking paper. Stick the paper down with blobs of meringue. Fold the dark cocoa powder through the meringue mixture, taking care not to lose any volume.

Spoon the mixture over the baking sheet, spreading it out evenly into a rough A4 rectangle shape. Bake for about 1 hour, or until the base of the meringue disc comes off the baking tray with ease. Let it cool - don't worry if it cracks, as you'll be smothering it with deliciousness.

While the meringue base is baking, prepare the poaching liquid. Bring the water to boil in a small heavy-bottomed pan, then add the sugar and cinnamon stick and bring to the boil again.

While the poaching liquid is heating up, peel the pears, core and slice into quarters, leaving the stalks on for effect. Carefully place the pears into the sugar syrup and poach gently for 15 minutes. Check the pears are soft by sticking a knife in them. Leave to poach a little longer if they are still hard. When they are ready, carefully lift out the pears with a slotted spoon, and set aside.

Carefully place the meringue disc on a rustic wooden board. Add a large pinch of sea salt to your dulce de leche (or caramel sauce). Get your creative juices flowing and dollop with mascarpone, swirl with the salted caramel, layer the pears and toasted walnuts over the meringue, then drizzle with the melted dark chocolate.

The meringue tray bake (without any toppings or sauces) will keep for 2 weeks, in an airtight container, stored in a cool, dry place.

DARK CHOCOLATE AND BLACKBERRY LAYER CAKE

SERVES 12

FOR THE CHOCOLATE DISKS:
800g caster sugar
400g free-range egg whites
   (approx 13 medium eggs)
4 tsp of cocoa
Extra cocoa to dust

FOR THE CREAM:
600ml double cream
1 tbsp icing sugar
1 tbsp crème de cassis or
   Chambord liqueur (optional)

FOR THE COULIS:
300g of blackberries (fresh or
   frozen), or any seasonal berries
1 tbsp of honey

FOR THE GANACHE:
200g 70% dark chocolate
300ml double cream

TO SERVE:
300g blackberries

This meringue cake has four layers of chocolate meringue discs, chocolate ganache and blackberry coulis and cream to make an indulgent dinner party centrepiece.

Preheat your oven to 100°C/gas ¼. Line 4 baking sheets with baking paper, and draw a 10 inch circle on each piece of paper.

Make your chocolate meringue mixture using the Meringue Girls method (*see p.26*), then divide it between the 4 circles, spreading it evenly to make 4 flat discs, roughly 1 inch thick. Dust all the discs with more cocoa so that they are covered in chocolate. Bake for 1 hour until dry, or until the base of the discs are firm and come cleanly off the paper. They are fragile as they are thin. These chocolate discs can be made up to 2 weeks in advance stored in an airtight cake tin.

To make the coulis, tip the blackberries into a heavy-bottomed pan, add the honey and a splash of water. Bring to the boil, then turn the heat down to a gentle simmer and cook for a further 5 minutes. Whiz in a food processor until smooth. Set aside to cool.

In a large bowl whisk the double cream and icing sugar together until it just holds its shape.

To make the ganache, break the chocolate into pieces and heat in the microwave or in a heatproof bowl set over a pan of simmering water, until just melted. Add the cream mixture and stir until it forms a thick & smooth ganache.

Start to layer the cake. Place 1 meringue disc on a cake stand or plate then, using a palette knife, spread a third of the chocolate ganache on the disc and top with a third of the cream, then, with the back of a knife, swirl some coulis through the cream to marble it. Add the second meringue disc and repeat the layers. Now add the final layer and dust with cocoa and scatter with fresh blackberries.

BOOZY WINTER ETON MESS

A boozy concoction of Cointreau-soaked clementines and brandy cream, mixed with meringue kisses and decorated with pomegranate seeds. This makes a fantastic alternative to traditional Christmas pudding.

SERVES 4

FOR THE CLEMENTINES:
300ml Cointreau
2 clementines, peeled
  and segmented

16 Meringue Kisses (see pp.30-35)

FOR THE BRANDY CREAM:
300ml double cream
2 tbsp icing sugar
A big splash of brandy, or to taste

TO DECORATE:
1 pomegranate, seeds bashed out
2 tbsp freeze-dried raspberries
  (optional)

For the clementines, pour the Cointreau into a bowl and add the clementine segments. Stir, making sure all the segments get coated with the alcohol, then cover and leave to soak in the fridge for at least 2 hours, or ideally overnight.

Make your Meringue Kisses (see pp.30-35).

For the brandy cream, pour the cream into a mixing bowl and add the icing sugar. Whisk until the cream is just thick, being very careful not to over-whisk. Add a big splash of brandy and fold into the whipped cream with a spoon.

Now you are ready to plate up. Spoon half the brandy cream onto the centre of a beautiful serving plate. Pile up your meringue kisses and then drizzle the rest of the brandy cream over the meringues. Decorate with the soaked clementines and the pomegranate seeds, then dust with finely chopped freeze-dried raspberries.

GIANT MERINGUES

Giant meringues nearly as big as your head! We hope that Ottolenghi, the godfather of meringues, would be proud of these displayed in his window.

MAKES 6 BIG ONES

1 batch of uncooked Meringue
 Girls Mixture (see p.26)
50g good-quality dark
 cocoa powder
50g cacao nibs
 (optional, can be bought from
 Holland & Barrett stores or
 online from Amazon sellers)
100g green pistachios,
 finely chopped

Preheat the oven to 100°C/gas ¼, and line 2 baking sheets with baking paper.

Make your meringue mixture (see p.26).

Fill a large plate with cocoa and cacao nibs, and another large plate with the finely chopped green pistachios

Taking half the meringue mixture, use 2 large metal spoons to roll 3 big blobs of meringue along the cocoa plate until they are nicely coated. Place on one of the baking sheets. Use the same technique with the rest of the mixture, and roll 3 big blobs of meringue along the pistachio plate. Place on the second baking sheet.

Bake for 3 hours, until the meringues easily come off the baking paper with their bases intact and they feel light and hollow when you tap the base. If they are still uncooked in the middle, turn the oven off and leave them in the oven for a few hours or overnight so that they continue to cook slowly.

Pile the meringues up in a big and impressive stack.

MAPLE MERINGUE-FILLED
CARAMELIZED BANANA DOUGHNUTS

Gosh, these are good. Doughnuts. Maple Meringue. Caramelized banana. Win.

MAKES 6

FOR THE DOUGHNUTS:

160g strong white flour, plus extra for dusting

7g packet of dried yeast

½ tsp salt

15g caster sugar

10g cinnamon, to dust

20g room temperature butter, chopped, plus extra for greasing

65ml whole milk, warmed

45ml warm water

1 free-range egg, beaten

2 litres of vegetable oil, to deep fry

FOR THE FILLING:

½ batch uncooked Maple Meringue mixture (see p.152)

FOR CINNAMON SUGAR:

2 tsp ground cinnamon

3 tbsp caster sugar

CAREMALIZED BANANAS:

2 bananas, sliced long ways

A splash of maple syrup

Combine the flour, yeast, salt and sugar in a large bowl and mix well. Put the butter into a bowl with the warm milk and water, and stir to melt. Pour this into the mixing bowl, along with the egg, and stir until it comes together. The dough should be firm, but soft.

Tip on to a lightly floured surface, or into a mixer fitted with a dough hook, and knead until smooth and stretchy (about 10 minutes). Put into a lightly greased bowl, cover with a damp tea towel, and leave in a warm place until doubled in size (about an hour).

Shape into 6 balls of about 80g each and put on a lightly floured baking tray, spacing them well apart. Cover and leave to rise again for 45 minutes.

Heat the oil in a large pan or deep-fat fryer to 160°C. Cook the doughnuts in 2 batches for about 3 minutes on each side, until golden, then blot with kitchen paper and sprinkle with caster sugar and cinnamon. Allow to cool slightly. Alternatively use good quality shop-bought plain doughnuts.

Meanwhile, make ½ a batch of Maple Meringue and fill a piping bag fitted with a small nozzle. Then make a small hole in the side of each doughnut and fill to the brim with the mixture.

Now caramelize your strips of banana by gently frying them in a pan with a splash of maple syrup. Lay banana strips over the doughnuts, and eat while hot.

SPICED APPLE CRUMBLE WITH CINNAMON MERINGUE KISSES AND WARM CUSTARD

This comforting winter-warmer pudding is a take on the classic apple crumble, with gooey Cinnamon Meringue Kisses and a contrasting salty crumble.

SERVES 4

16 Cinnamon Meringue Kisses
  (*see pp.30 & 33*)

FOR THE SALTED CRUMBLE:
50g butter, at room temperature
50g plain flour
50g golden caster sugar
1 tsp flaked sea salt
25g flaked almonds

FOR THE STEWED APPLES:
4 Bramley cooking apples, peeled,
  cored and roughly chopped
1 tbsp dark brown sugar
Pinch of cinnamon powder

600g Vanilla Custard (*see p.143*),
  or use a carton of good-quality
  ready-made custard

Make your Cinnamon Meringue Kisses (*see pp.30 & 33*).

Preheat the oven to 180°C/gas 4.

For the salted crumble, sift the flour, sugar and salt into a mixing bowl. Add the butter and, using your fingertips, mix well until the mixture resembles breadcrumbs. Stir in the flaked almonds.

Scatter the crumble mixture on a baking tray and bake for 15 minutes, tossing occasionally until the crumble is golden brown. Leave to cool (it will harden as it cools).

For the stewed apples, place the apple chunks in a pan. Add a splash of water, the dark brown sugar and cinnamon powder, and gently stew until soft, but not mushy.

Just before serving, make the Vanilla Custard (*see p.143.*), or heat your ready-made custard.

To plate up, divide the steaming stewed apples between 4 small bowls and top with 4 Cinnamon Meringue Kisses per bowl. Sprinkle with lots of salted crumble and pour the hot custard over. Serve immediately.

Gift IDEAS

CHEWY PISTACHIO COFFEE DUNKERS

The ultimate coffee dunker, these have a crisp outside and chewy middle, with a delicate green colour and deep pistachio taste. Cut into any shape you like, we used our MG cookie cutters, and dunked into our favourite mug.

MAKES 12 COOKIES

1 batch of uncooked Meringue
   Girls Mixture (see p.26)
1 tsp vanilla extract
1 tsp white wine vinegar
350g shelled pistachios,
   finely ground

Preheat the oven to 190°C/gas 5. Line a Swiss roll tin, or small shallow baking tray with greased baking paper.

Make a batch of stiff and glossy meringue mixture (see p.26). Carefully fold in 1 tsp vanilla extract, 1 tsp vinegar (the vinegar is what gives it a lovely chewy middle), and then ground pistachios.

Spoon the mixture into the lined tin, carefully spreading it out from the middle until it is roughly 2cm thick all over.

Bake for 30–40 minutes, until the top of the meringue is crisp and golden and the middle is still a bit gooey. It will harden a little further once it cools.

Turn out onto a wire rack to cool, and peel off the baking paper.

When completely cool, use a cookie cutter to press out shapes. These make a lovely gift, and last well for 1 week in an airtight biscuit tin.

EASTER EGG BOX

Make egg-shaped sandwiched kisses for a home-made Easter gift. This is a fun activity to do with kids. These eggs are made by sandwiching 2 meringue shells together with melted chocolate and then dusting with cocoa to give a speckled egg appearance. Choose any flavour from the kiss flavourings on p.32-35, or keep them plain as we've done.

MAKES ABOUT 12 EASTER EGGS

½ batch of uncooked Meringue Girls Mixture *(see p.26)*
A few drops of natural food colouring in your chosen colour
A pinch of cocoa, to dust

FOR THE CHOCOLATE GANACHE:

50g 70% dark chocolate
50ml double cream

Preheat the oven to 100°C/gas ¼, and line a baking sheet with baking paper.

Make ½ a batch of meringue mixture, *(see p.26)*. Then fold through a few drops of natural food colouring to make a light pastel shade. Fill a disposable piping bag with the meringue mixture and cut a 2.5cm hole in the tip.

Pipe about 24 small dollops of meringue mixture onto the lined baking sheet until all the mixture is used up. Then, with a damp finger, carefully press down and round the tips of the meringue peaks so you have a smoother 'eggshell' shape. Dust with a few specks of cocoa powder.

Bake for 30-40 minutes, or until the meringues come off the baking paper easily with their bases intact. Leave to cool.

Break the chocolate into pieces and gently melt in a heatproof bowl set over a pan of simmering water or in a micro-safe bowl in the microwave. Once the chocolate has melted, gently fold in the double cream until you have a thick, smooth paste.

Using a knife, spread the base of each kiss with chocolate and then sandwich 2 together to form an egg shape. Repeat with the remaining kisses.

Put your meringue eggs in an egg cup or egg box and tie each box with a ribbon and a feather. Or use some straw to make your own little 'nests' for them to nestle in. The meringue eggs will keep for 2 weeks in an airtight container.

MERINGUE ALPHABET

Why stick to piping kisses? Get creative with letters of the alphabet. Bake the letters of a friend's name, or a personal message like 'Happy Birthday'. These are great for a wedding dessert table – 'Congratulations Mr & Mrs' – as well as kids' parties or big romantic gestures. You could also make the letters smaller to decorate the top of a cake. Remember that the letters will expand a bit in the oven, but this just adds to their home-made charm. Here, we've gone all out with different coloured rainbow letters – just because.

MAKES ENOUGH
FOR ABOUT 15
LARGE LETTERS

1 batch of uncooked Meringue
   Girls Mixture (*see p.26*)
Colours of your choice,
   we used Wilton Gels
   for a stronger colour

Preheat the oven to 100°C/gas ¼, and line 3 baking sheets with baking paper.

Make your meringue mixture (*see p.26*). To colour your letters, instead of painting stripes, paint the entire inside top tip of a disposable piping bag with your chosen colour. Then fill with meringue mixture. Cut a small 5p-sized hole in the tip. To make different coloured letters use separate piping bags and colours.

With your creative juices flowing, pipe out your chosen letters on the lined baking sheets. Leave enough space between the letters to allow them to expand without touching each other.

Bake for 1 hour until they are very firm and they lift off the baking paper with ease. Remember that they are fragile. Get spelling.

USING YOUR YOLKS

PASSION FRUIT CURD

Use this zingy Passion Fruit Curd for the passion fruit pie filling on p.107. It's also divine on toasted crumpets. The curd will keep well in sterilised jars for up to 2 weeks in the fridge.

MAKES 500G

160ml passion fruit pulp, or use shop-bought (available in jars)
1 tbsp fresh lemon juice
165g chilled unsalted butter, cut into cubes
200g caster sugar
5 egg yolks

Place the passion fruit pulp, lemon juice, butter and sugar in a medium-sized, heavy-bottomed saucepan over a medium heat and stir until the butter has melted and the sugar has dissolved.

Place the egg yolks in a bowl and whisk until combined. Gradually add the passion fruit mixture to the egg yolks, whisking continuously.

Return the curd mixture to the pan over a low heat, and cook, stirring, for 6-7 minutes, or until the mixture is thick enough to coat the back of a spoon.

Leave to cool. If not using immediately, cover with cling film or put in an airtight container and store in the fridge for up to 2 weeks.

This makes enough curd for a large passion fruit meringue pie (substitute for the Lemongrass and Chilli Curd in the receipe on p.84) or 12 Mini Passion Fruit Filo Meringue Pies (*see p.107*).

NOTE: It is important to sterilise any jars used to remove bacteria - dirty jars will quickly spoil whatever food you put in them. To sterilise your jars and their lids, put them in your dishwasher and begin making your curd. (Alternatively heat your oven to 180°C/gas 4, place the jars on oven trays, making sure the jars don't touch each other, and heat for at least 20 minutes.) When the curd is ready, remove the jars one by one so that they stay hot and fill them with hot curd. Do not put cold food into hot jars or hot food into cold jars - the glass could shatter.

LEMONGRASS AND CHILLI CURD

We LOVE this Lemongrass and Chilli Curd. Both tangy and creamy, it's one of life's simple pleasures. Curd is a great staple to have in your kitchen, ready to jazz up any dessert. Make it on a rainy day and keep it in the fridge, or give to friends as a home-made gift.

MAKES 500G

1 Stick of lemongrass
  (bruised with a knife)
1 Red Chilli, sliced down
  the centre (optional)
Zest and juice of 2
  unwaxed lemons
225g caster sugar
60g chilled unsalted butter,
  cut into cubes
2 eggs, plus 2 egg yolk
1 tsp Cornstarch

Put the lemongrass, chilli, lemon zest and juice, butter and sugar into a saucepan over a medium heat until butter has melted and sugar has completely dissolved. Strain through a sieve into a clean bowl.

Lightly whisk the eggs and the egg yolks in a separate bowl. Slowly pour the lemongrass (or plain lemon) mixture through the egg mixture whisking franticly ensuring the eggs don't scramble. Whisk until all of the ingredients are well combined. In a separate bowl, mix the cornstarch with a splash of water and whisk until there are zero lumps. Add this to the curd mixture and put back on the stove top over a low heat, stirring continuously until the curd thickens and is creamy enough to coat the back of a spoon.

Remove the lemon curd from the heat and set aside to cool, stirring occasionally as it cools. Once cooled, spoon the lemon curd into sterilised jars (*see Note on p.139*), and seal. Keep in the fridge until ready to use.

To make ordinary Lemon Curd leave out the lemongrass and the chilli.

CHEAT'S CURD

The easiest way to make delicious curd fillings. So simple and quick, it works a treat. We've stayed with the classic lemon curd, but feel free to substitute the lemon juice with any citrus flavour you like.

3 egg yolks
1 large tin (397g) of
 condensed milk
Juice and zest of 4 unwaxed
 lemons (grapefruit, blood
 orange or lime will work too)

Put the yolks in a bowl and beat with an electric whisk for 2 minutes. Add the condensed milk and whisk for another 3 minutes, then add the lemon juice and zest and continue to whisk for another 4 minutes.

Pour into a 20cm tart base and bake at 160°C/gas 3 for 15 minutes, or until just set.

VANILLA CUSTARD

This classic vanilla custard recipe is a great way to use up any spare egg yolks. Although it takes a bit of effort, you can't beat the taste of home-made custard – just like mama used to make...

MAKES 600ML

570ml milk
55ml single cream
1 vanilla pod, split with seeds scraped out
4 egg yolks
30g caster sugar
2 tsp cornflour

To infuse the flavours, bring the milk, cream and split vanilla pod and seeds to simmering point in a saucepan over a low heat. Once the flavour of the vanilla has infused, fish out the pod.

In a separate bowl, whisk the egg yolks, sugar and cornflour together and slowly pour the hot milk and cream over them, whisking continuously.

Put the mixture back in the saucepan and simmer over a low heat, stirring constantly with a wooden spoon. Using the wooden spoon, feel the base of the pan for a silky texture so that you know that the custard is beginning to thicken.

Once the custard has thickened enough to coat the back of the spoon, take off the heat and strain through a sieve to remove any lumps.

Serve immediately, or if you want to keep the custard hot for a while, pour into a jug, cover with cling film and leave in a warm bain-marie.

LYONS

CAKES

other
MERINGUE
methods

MARSHMALLOW
MERINGUE

A really gooey meringue recipe. When chilled, the marshmallows set the meringue mixture so you get a really mallowy, thick and gooey texture. Delicious on the no-bake pretzel chocolate tart on p.105, or as a topping for any sweet tart or cake.

MAKES 415G

10 marshmallows,
  melted in a microwave
150g free-range egg whites
  (5 medium eggs)
300g caster sugar

Start by lining a large baking sheet with baking paper.

Preheat the oven to 200°C/gas 6. Line a roasting tray with baking paper, pour in the caster sugar and put in the oven for about 5 minutes until the edges are just beginning to melt. Heating the sugar will help it dissolve in the egg whites more quickly to create a glossy, stable mixture.

Meanwhile, weigh your egg whites in your free-standing mixer bowl, or a non-plastic bowl. Make sure your bowl and whisk are free from grease. Whisk slowly at first, allowing small stabilising bubbles to form, then increase the speed until the egg whites form stiff peaks, and the bowl can be tipped upside down without the egg falling out.

Keep an eye on the mixture and stop whisking just before it turns into a cotton woolly appearance, meaning that the mixture has over-whisked and lost some elasticity in the egg white protein.

At this point, the sugar should be ready to take out of the oven. Turn your oven down to 100°C/gas ¼. Leave the door ajar to speed up the cooling.

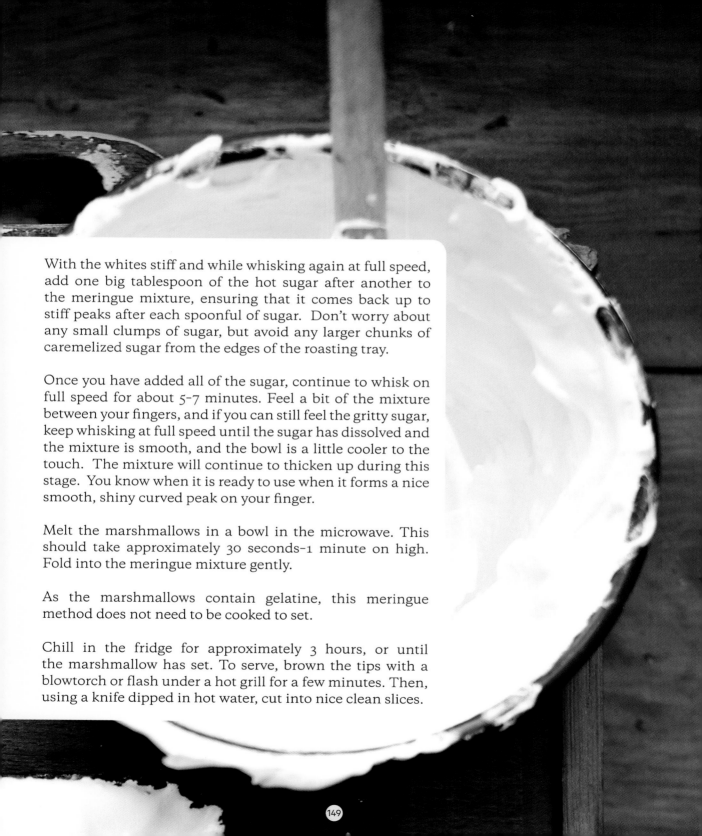

With the whites stiff and while whisking again at full speed, add one big tablespoon of the hot sugar after another to the meringue mixture, ensuring that it comes back up to stiff peaks after each spoonful of sugar. Don't worry about any small clumps of sugar, but avoid any larger chunks of caremelized sugar from the edges of the roasting tray.

Once you have added all of the sugar, continue to whisk on full speed for about 5-7 minutes. Feel a bit of the mixture between your fingers, and if you can still feel the gritty sugar, keep whisking at full speed until the sugar has dissolved and the mixture is smooth, and the bowl is a little cooler to the touch. The mixture will continue to thicken up during this stage. You know when it is ready to use when it forms a nice smooth, shiny curved peak on your finger.

Melt the marshmallows in a bowl in the microwave. This should take approximately 30 seconds-1 minute on high. Fold into the meringue mixture gently.

As the marshmallows contain gelatine, this meringue method does not need to be cooked to set.

Chill in the fridge for approximately 3 hours, or until the marshmallow has set. To serve, brown the tips with a blowtorch or flash under a hot grill for a few minutes. Then, using a knife dipped in hot water, cut into nice clean slices.

ITALIAN MERINGUE

The Italian Meringue method involves making a sugar syrup, which is then added to the stiff egg whites to partially cook the meringue on the spot. There is no need for baking, so this is a great mixture to use as a topping, as for the Lemongrass and Chilli Meringue Pie on p.84 and the Mini Passion Fruit Filo Meringue Pies on p.107. It also makes a great filling as for the Lemon Meringue Waffles on p.91.

225g granulated sugar
6 tbsp water
120g egg whites (4 eggs)

Pour the sugar and water into a heavy-bottomed saucepan. Slowly bring to the boil, stirring occasionally with a wooden spoon.

Have a pastry brush and a cup of cold water to hand, and if any sugar crystals get stuck at the side of the pan, brush them down into the syrup. If you let them build up, they will attract all the other bits of sugar and the sugar won't dissolve well.

The syrup is ready is ready when it reaches 120°C. To check this, use a sugar thermometer if you have one, or use the 'firm ball' technique. For the latter, drop a teaspoon of the syrup into the cup of cold water. If the syrup has reached 120°C, it will set into a firm ball, which can be squashed between your fingers. If the syrup forms a hard ball, like a hard-boiled sweet, it has reached too high a temperature for making Italian meringue – take it off the heat for 2 minutes or so to bring it back down to the appropriate temperature. If it just dissolves into the water, it is not yet hot enough.

While the syrup is boiling, whisk the egg whites to stiff peaks.

If you haven't got a free-standing electric whisk, you will need 2 people to do the next stage as you need to keep whisking the whites as you pour the syrup over them. The syrup must be bubbling hot as it hits the whites in order to partially cook them. So, carefully pour the bubbling hot syrup onto the whites in a steady stream, all the while continuing to whisk. Take care not to pour the syrup onto the wires of the whisk as it will quickly cool against the cold metal and can then harden and stick to the whisk.

Once you've added all the syrup, whisk hard and fast until the mixture is stiff, shiny and cooled, which will take 5-7 minutes. When it's ready, the meringue should not flow off the whisk when the whisk is lifted.

Use to top your meringue pie or pies or to fill your lemon waffles. If using as a pie topping, blow-torch the peaks or flash under a hot grill until golden.

MAPLE MERINGUE

This Maple Meringue uses natural maple syrup instead of refined sugar. Similar to an Italian meringue, you heat the maple syrup to a high temperature and add it to the stiff egg whites. The earthy and rich maple flavour really comes through in this recipe. The mixture doesn't need to be baked, so is perfect for our banana doughnuts on p.119. It also works really well in recipes for baked meringues or a pavlova or as a filling for waffles.

MAKES 350G

240ml maple syrup
120g egg whites (4 egg whites)

You will need a sugar
  thermometer for this recipe

Put the maple syrup in heavy-bottomed pan along with a sugar thermometer. Place the pan over a medium heat.

When the syrup approaches 105°C, place the egg whites in the bowl of a free-standing mixer and mix until just frothy. Then increase to full speed and beat until the whites can hold a stiff peak.

When the syrup has come up to 113°C, put the mixer back on medium speed and slowly stream in the hot maple syrup, continuing to beat until the meringue is thick and a little shiny. This will take about 5–7 minutes.

Use to fill the doughnuts on p.119. If you want to make these into kisses, turn to p.30. They will keep for 2 weeks, covered with cling film or placed in an airtight container and stored in a cool dry place.

Stacey Loves

DMS & LONG SKIRTS
Charity Shop Bargains
3 SUGARS IN A TEA
Red Lippy
Japanese Anime
AND BJORK

Alex Loves

BOSTON TERRIERS
Gold Disco Pants
FOOD STYLING
Car Boot Sale Foraging
VINTAGE KITCHENALIA
& Pomegranate Prosecco

SCAN WITH
layar
SEE PAGE 4
for instructions

INDEX

We would like to thank...

DAVID LOFTUS, undoubtably the world's best food photographer, for believing in the underdogs and for educating us on the rules of Instagram etiquette! This book would be nowhere near as beautiful without you.

A BIG thank you to all the team at SQUARE PEG, especially ROWAN YAPP for her belief in us and our occasional off the wall ideas!

DOUG KERR and GEMMA GERMAINS from our brilliant design team at WELL MADE STUDIO, who hit the nail on the head, and also KENN GOODALL for the painted titles.

Alex's parents, NICKY STEPHENSON & LAURIE HOFFLER aka MUMMA & PAPA LOUIGI. Thank you for everything, I love you both more than the Universe.

Stacey's parents, SUE & BRENDAN O'GORMAN aka MAMA GORM & PAPA GORM, for their never-ending support from a far. Also, GRANDMA & GRANDPA BLAIR for their generosity and AUNTIE CAROL for her award-winning recipe development ideas.

TIM ETCHELLS for all his fantastic advice and for putting the MG wheels in motion...

SIAN O'GORMAN, for being the best sister in the world, for her creative genius and eye for design, and for being the creator of the Meringue Girls logo.

NEIL 'REAL' BURNELL for all your love and support over 8 wonderful years, and for keeping the bed warm for me after long nights of baking.

BRADY POLKIE for always keeping my spirits up. I am the luckiest girl in the world.

NICO RILLA our incredibly supportive head chef (and second Dad), the Meringue Girls would not exist without you.

To all the teachers at LEITHS SCHOOL OF FOOD & WINE for their fantastic training, and to all the LEITHS' STUDENTS that have helped us along the way.

GIZZI ERSKINE, for seeing something in us, and always having our back.

JO HARRIS at TOPHAM STREET, for her incredible eye for style and general loveliness.

CLAIRE STRICKETT (our first ever MG employee!) For not only being a pro meringue maker, but for her general amazingness and helping us in all aspects of the business.

MELISSA BAKTH at SQUASH BANANA DESIGNS for our beautiful website, and continued support.

ANDY FERNANDEZ, for her exquiste hand modelling and help on the book shoot.

DEAN BRETTSCHNEIDER, the master baker, thank you for giving us the time to pick your brains, and for all your mentoring advice.

MARTYN and the whole team at HAPPY KITCHEN for so generously sharing their space with us.

MATT YOUNG aka VAN BLANC, the classiest white van man in town.

DENIS from DENEEMOTION, for our wonderful videos.

BECCA GRAHAM, the best PR girl you could ever wish for, and the best chance meeting on Gumtree.

ASHLEE ACKLAND, for your incredible data entry skills and general awesomeness.

Meringue Girls x